Simple Sermons for Funeral Services

Simple Sermons for Funeral Services

W. Herschel Ford

Baker Books

A Division of Baker Book House Co
Grand Rapids, Michigan 49516

Published by Baker Books
a division of Baker Book House Company
P.O. Box 6287, Grand Rapids, MI 49516-6287

New edition published 2001

First reprinted 1985 by Baker Book House Company with the permission of the copyright holder.

Printed in the United States of America

ISBN 0-8010-9122-5

Scripture is taken from the King James Version of the Bible.

Chapter 9 is taken from W. Herschel Ford's *Simple Sermons on Grace and Glory* (Grand Rapids: Zondervan, 1977).

For current information about all releases from Baker Book House, visit our web site:
http://www.bakerbooks.com

This little book is lovingly dedicated to the memory of my dear friend, Rube M. Evans, a wonderful man of God who is now in the glory world, and in deep appreciation for his beloved companion, Mrs. Mary Evans, who has been a great blessing to me and many others, through her sweet spirit and beautiful life and generous help.

Contents

Preface

Each message is given as if the talk were being delivered at the funeral of some particular person. Ministers can change the thoughts to fit the occasion. If you find some truths repeated in these messages, it is because it seemed that these repeated truths were appropriate for that particular service.

I would suggest that some of the following Scriptures be used for your funeral messages.

John 14:1–3, 27	1 Corinthians 15:51–58
2 Timothy 4:6–8	1 Thessalonians 4:13–18
Romans 8:37–39	Revelation 7:9–17
2 Corinthians 5:1	Revelation 14:13
Matthew 11:28	Revelation 21:1–4
Psalm 23	2 Samuel 12:15–23

I trust that these simple messages will help my preacher brethren to bring comfort to the bereaved, glory to God, and souls to the Savior.

W. Herschel Ford

1

For a Christian Man

We are always to remember that our funeral services are not for the dead, but for the living. There is no word that we can say that can reach the ear of our friend. There is no music, however sweet, that can touch his heart. And, although we would pay a tribute to him and his faithful Christian life, this service is primarily for those who are gathered here today out of love and respect for a good man.

The great question that comes to mind when one dies is this: "Was he ready to go?" We thank God that our friend settled this matter many years ago when he repented of his sins and trusted Jesus Christ as his personal Savior. And since that time he has served Christ well, always being true and faithful to the Lord, to his church, and to the highest and best things of life.

I. The Bible Says Many Wonderful Things about the Death of a Christian

We hear these words, "Blessed are the dead which die in the Lord, for they rest from their labors and their works do follow them." The word "blessed" here means "happy." Not all those who die are going to be happy, but those who die "in the Lord" will come to know the supreme happiness that only God can give. Then we read, "Precious in the sight of the Lord is the death of his saints." Now, according to the Bible, every child of God is a saint. And every movement of the Christian's life is precious in God's sight. Then surely, when his people die, it is precious in God's sight. John Wesley said on the occasion, "Our people die well."

Again we read, "He giveth his beloved sleep." Elizabeth Barrett Browning said that to her this was the sweetest verse in the Bible. We struggle and strain, we worry and fret through this life. We become tired and worn out. And then God puts us to sleep for a while and we wake up in glory. Again we read, "Absent from the body, present with the Lord." The body is put away in the grave, but the real person, the spirit, the soul is not there. The Christian has simply left his old worn-out body down here and has gone out to be with the Lord. Isn't that wonderful? "Absent from the body, present with the Lord." Frankly, we'll be glad to get rid of this old sinful, sick, weary body when that day comes.

II. What Does a Christian Gain by Dying?

Paul said, "For me to live is Christ and to die is gain." Does a man gain anything when he dies? Doesn't he have to leave everything behind, his home, his loved ones, his friends? Yes, that is true, but he can know that he will gain infinitely more in death than he can ever gain in this life.

1. He gains freedom

Freedom from all the aches and pains and sorrows and suffering and problems and troubles of this world. Some years ago I was called to the bedside of my father, who was critically ill. I sat by that bedside all through the night and the next day at noon, as I held his hand, my father slipped away to be with God. And I bowed my head and thanked God that my father was free from pain and sorrow and had gone home to heaven, where these things could never touch him again. Yes—we gain freedom when we die in Christ.

2. He gains fellowship

The Christian in dying gains the sweetest fellowship ever enjoyed by anyone. Fellowship with all the great men and women of the Bible. Fellowship with all the great people of all ages. Fellowship with all the loved ones whom we "have loved long since and lost awhile." And best of all, fellowship with the Lord Jesus Christ, who made heaven possible for us.

Oh, the dear ones in glory, how they beckon me to come, and our parting at the river I recall, To the sweet vales of Eden they shall sing my welcome home, But I long to see my Savior first of all.

3. He gains fullness of knowledge

Oh, there are so many things down here that we don't understand. We wonder why sin comes in to break our hearts and blast our hopes. We wonder why so often some fine and useful person is taken away and another is left who makes no contribution to the world's benefit. We will never understand these things down here, but someday in the golden glow of that better land we'll sit down beside the Lord Jesus and he will explain it all. Then we will see that some of the things that caused us so much sorrow down here were simply blessings in disguise, and God allowed them to come to us for our good and his glory.

Not now, but in the coming years, It may be in the better land, We'll read the meaning of our tears, And there, sometime, we'll understand.

III. Lessons for the Living

1. Death is certain

If the Lord tarries, if he doesn't return in our lifetime, we shall all die. "It is appointed unto man once to die, and after that the judgment." Death may come soon to some of us, it will not surely be long for any of us. It may come suddenly or it may come after a lingering illness. It comes to the king's palace, it comes to the poor man's cottage. But it is coming and we must get ready for it.

2. The one way to prepare for death

There is only one way to prepare for death and the judgment. That is through faith in the Lord Jesus Christ. There is no other way of salvation. "He that believeth on the Son hath everlasting life: and he that believeth on the Son shall not see life; but the wrath of God abideth on him."

IV. Your Comfort in This Hour

1. You are comforted in remembering that you did your best for your loved one

You gave him the best medical skill and nursing care that could be given anyone. Now you can say with one of old, "The Lord gave and the Lord hath taken away; blessed be the name of the Lord."

2. You are comforted in remembering that death isn't all

Beyond this vale of tears there is another life and another land. The grave is not our goal. We look forward to a new home of joy and bliss that will be ours when we leave this earthly home.

3. You are comforted in remembering that you will see your loved one again

The Bible certainly implies that we shall see and know our loved ones in heaven. David said that he could not bring his baby back to this earth, but that he could go to him. Heaven is a complete place, but would it be entirely complete if we never saw our loved ones up there? Surely, surely, we will see them again in a land where we will know even as we are known.

4. But our greatest comfort comes from Christ

One day he spoke to a group of people just like us and he said, "Come unto me, all ye that labor and are heavy laden and I will give you rest." He stands today with open arms and says the same thing to you. Just come to him, lean your head on his bosom, and he will give you the rest and the comfort and the grace and the courage you need for this hour.

One of our ladies recently underwent a serious and delicate throat operation. Later I asked her to tell me about it. And she said, "When they rolled me out of my hospital room and toward the operating room, I just closed my eyes and turned it all over to God and he gave me peace and brought me safely through." So I bid you today to turn all your sorrow over to Jesus. He will bring you safely through, giving you grace and comfort for today and courage for all of your tomorrows.

So may God bless the memory of this good man. And may he bless and comfort all of you who mourn today. And may all of us place our hands in the nail-pierced hand of Jesus and follow him until he takes us home.

2

For a Christian Woman

A busy pastor conducts many funerals. I recently conducted the funeral of a woman 103 years of age; I have conducted funeral services for many babies; I have conducted services for the poor people who were buried by the county; I have conducted services for those who had been murdered and for those who had committed suicide.

The preacher must always keep a tender and sympathetic heart. Funeral services must never become mechanical or matter-of-fact with him. But some funeral services come closer home to the preacher than others. Such is the case on this occasion as we come to say our farewells to this consecrated Christian woman, whose life meant so much to our church, to others, and to ourselves.

I. The Only Thing That Matters

When you come to the end of your life there is only one thing that counts. It doesn't matter how much money you've made nor how high you have risen in the social circle. It doesn't matter how large a house you have lived in. It doesn't matter how many friends you had or how many flowers bedeck your casket. The only thing that matters is your relationship to God through faith in the Lord Jesus Christ. If he is your Savior, all is well. If not, there is no hope for you. It is a tragedy to be born into the world and not to be born again through faith in Christ.

Now our dear friend settled this matter long ago. She gave her heart and life to Christ and she served him well to the end. She was never rich. She didn't live in a costly mansion. She never rose to a high social position. But the true riches in Christ were hers, and at the end of the way she inherited greater possessions than any man in this world ever had.

II. What Shall I Say of Her Life?

1. It was a life of helpfulness

Like her Master, she went about doing good. She touched many lives with her good deeds. She blessed many hearts because of her kind words. She lifted many people closer to God through her own consecrated Christian life.

2. It was a life of humility

Although she went out of her way and beyond the call of duty to help others, she never boasted about it. She always kept in the background, willing always that others should have the credit and that God should have the glory. She could say with John the Baptist, "I must decrease, but Christ must increase."

3. It was a life of faithfulness

Jesus said, "Be thou faithful unto death and I will give thee a crown of life." She was faithful and now she has gone on to receive that crown. The Lord and her church could always count on her. She was always at her place in every service of the church. It can be truly said of her that she sought first the kingdom of God and his righteousness.

She engaged in the work of other fine worthwhile organizations, but always the work of her Lord took precedence over everything else. When you have said that a Christian is faithful, you have said the best thing that can be said about him. She was faithful, faithful to all that is highest and best.

4. It was a life that leaves a precious memory

During all the days that are left to her loved ones, they will be having many sweet memories of her. These memories will bless and enrich them forever. They will remember the worthwhile things she said and the unselfish things she did. Their lives will be richer and they will be drawn closer to God because of these memories.

5. It was a life that tells of a blessed hope

When a Christian leaves us, it is not forever. We have a hope, a hope of another life, where we shall be with Jesus and where we shall see our loved ones again. "If in this life only, we have hope in Christ, we are of all men most miserable." But we have this hope, a blessed and wonderful thing. If this life is all, it isn't worth the candle. So we thank God for a hope that is steadfast and true.

III. The Mystery and Meaning of Death

Surely we can never understand why God takes away someone so noble and useful as our friend, but we know his way is the best way. The death of his saints is precious in his sight. "All things work together for good to them that love God." If a Christian lives for Christ, it is gain to die. This is just God's way of translating his children from a world of sorrow to a heaven of bliss.

IV. The Assurance Needed in This Hour

Many people have no assurance that all will be well when death comes. But in Christ we have assurance. We know he'll be with us in the hour of death and take us safely across the river. We can say with David, "Though I walk through the valley of the shadow of death, I will fear no evil, for Thou art with me, Thy rod and Thy staff they comfort me."

There is only one way to obtain this assurance. It must come from our faith in Christ. It must come from living for him and for the things that really count. Too many people are giving their lives for the things that die with the setting sun. Those who trust Christ and live their lives for him will have the needed assurance when they come to the dark valley.

A little girl said when she lay dying, "I don't see a valley. I just see Jesus." That's where our assurance lies.

So let us be thankful for a life well-lived, a life devoted to goodness, to faith in Christ, to unselfish service. And let us be thankful for a God of all grace, who is with us in life and in death and throughout eternity.

In my first pastorate I learned that one of our young women was critically ill in the hospital. I went over to see her, but as I walked up the steps I met a friend who told me that the young woman had just died. Two days later I was to conduct her funeral. I went out to the home just before we were to go to the church and the cemetery. I went through the front room, by the casket and the flowers and the friends, and into the back room to speak to the young woman's mother.

I took her hand in mine and tried to say some words of comfort to her. But I did not need to say anything. She put both her hands on mine and said, "Pastor, what would I do now without Jesus?" And I wonder what you and I would do in our homes of sorrow if we didn't have him.

May God help us all to find our comfort and our strength in him until at last we see him and our loved ones face to face.

3

For One Who Has Met a Tragic Death

This life is filled with many mysteries. It is not meant for us to understand everything. We would be as wise as God if we did. The tragedy connected with this funeral is fresh in our minds. We have been saying, "Why did this happen?" I cannot give you the answer. We'll never understand it in this world. Maybe God is saying to us, "Not now, but later. Someday you'll understand that even this was a blessing in disguise."

David's baby lay desperately ill. So David fell before the Lord and pled with God to spare the child. But God saw fit to take the baby away. Then David cleaned himself, put on his best clothes, and went to church and worshiped God. He then returned home and sat down to eat. His servants wondered why he could so soon return to the normal routine of life and he said, "I prayed for the baby, but for some reason God permitted him to die. Now I don't understand it all, but I must accept God's will. I can't bring the baby back, but I can go to him."

You need to do what David did. He went to church and worshiped God. Some people quit church altogether when sorrow comes. But in so doing they rob themselves of their sweetest source of strength and comfort. David also prayed. Sorrow ought to bring us to our knees. If there is any time when we need to pray and seek God's face, it is in the hour of sorrow.

Then David submitted to God's will. He said in effect, "I don't understand it, but I humbly bow to the will of God. Though he slay me, yet will I trust him." And David returned to his activities knowing the comfort that comes to one who is busy for the Lord.

I. The Acceptance of Mysteries

We accept many of the material mysteries of life without question. We don't understand how a picture and a sound can travel through a small wire into our livingrooms, but we don't throw out our televisions, although we don't understand them. We don't understand how a space shuttle can travel in orbit around the earth at a speed of more than 300 miles per minute, but we know it has happened and we accept it.

Now why can't we accept the spiritual mysteries of life? Why can't we trust when we don't understand? After all, that is what we need to do most of all today.

II. All Things Working Together

Paul says that "we know all things work together for good to them that love God." This doesn't mean that all things are good. Some things are tragically bad and heartbreaking. But God knows how to mix all the ingredients of life. He puts them all together, the good and the bad, and he causes it all to work out for our benefit and blessing. I know it's hard to see this today, but in God's own good time he'll make it clear and we'll understand.

III. Christ's Gracious Invitation to All

He invites us all to come to him. This word "come" seems to be God's favorite word.

1. Come to him for salvation

We can find salvation nowhere else except in Christ. "There is no other name given under heaven among men whereby we must be saved." He promises that he will cleanse and forgive and save us if we come to him. This is the first and most important duty of life. This matter must be settled before any other matter in life.

2. Come to him for comfort

Jesus said, "Come unto me all ye that labor and are heavy laden and I will give you rest." Surely he is speaking here especially to those who are in sorrow. This means that he is talking directly to you. The tender Shepherd, the God of all grace, opens his loving arms and invites you to come and find comfort in him.

3. Come to him at the end of the way

If Christ is yours, you need not fear death. He'll be there waiting to carry you home. You will hear him say: "Come ye blessed of my father, inherit the kingdom prepared for you from the foundation of the world."

Some years ago a couple in our city went hunting on a Sunday. When they returned home on Sunday night they put their gun in its usual place, leaving it still loaded. Then on Monday night when they came home from work, they found their 12-year-old son and his grandmother lying dead on the floor, with the gun beside them. It was thought that maybe someone else had entered the house and killed them or that possibly the boy had accidentally killed his grandmother and then in remorse had shot himself.

I conducted the double funeral and did all I could to bring comfort to the stricken parents. I visited them in their home, also, and talked and prayed with them. In a few Sundays they both came forward in the church, professing their faith in Christ and asking for baptism and church membership. They became wonderful Christians and faithful church members. From that time on, Sunday became for them a holy day and not a day for worldly sports. They brought their sorrow to Jesus and he not only gave them his glorious salvation, but he comforted their hearts and assuaged their grief.

Jesus invites all who mourn today to come to him for comfort. We'll do all we can to help you. But we are only human, after all. Only Christ can help in this hour. Let me urge you to turn the whole thing over to him.

May God bless you in this hour and lead you into the peace that passeth all understanding.

4

For a Baby or a Small Child

We read in God's Book that "Jesus called a little child unto himself." That was in the long, long ago when he walked here among men. He wanted to teach a lesson in humility, so he took that child in his arms and told his disciples that one must become as a little child and be converted before he could enter into the kingdom of heaven.

I can imagine Jesus, with his loving arms around that little child, fondling its pretty face and smiling down into its eyes. You see, Jesus loved little children, so he called this one to him. And last Monday morning Jesus came to your city and again he called a little child unto himself.

I. He Loves Little Children

You loved this little one. She has been a joy to your hearts. She has been a bright light in your home. But Jesus loved her, too, and now she has gone to light up his heavenly home and to bring joy to his heart. We will never think of her as being in a cemetery, but up there in heaven with the One who loved little children and who said, "Suffer the little children and forbid them not to come unto me, for of such is the kingdom of heaven."

Life can be compared to a rose garden. In this garden there are many varieties and sizes of roses. Some of them are full-blown, while some of them are just little buds. Now when the owner of the garden wants a bouquet for his table, he goes out into the garden and plucks those roses which will make the loveliest bouquet. He may pluck a full-blown rose or a little bud. The choice is his. And when God wants a bouquet for the heavenly table, the choice is up to him. He owns the garden and he picks the flowers as he chooses. Sometimes it's the full-blown flower of an aged person, but last Monday he picked a bright little bud to beautify the heavenly table.

And life can be compared to a school. Some people finish only the elementary grades, while others go ahead and finish high school and college and university. And some people in life's school finish only a few years of life and God calls them home, while others live on and learn many more of life's lessons before they graduate into heaven. Now your little one won't have to go all the way through life's school with all of its hardships. God has already said, "It is enough," and has called her home.

David had a sorrow like yours. When his baby boy died his heart was broken. But he did not weep as one who had no comfort. He said that he couldn't bring the baby back but that he could live for God in such a way as to be able to go to the baby someday. Maybe that's God's message for someone here today.

Some years ago I was called on to conduct the funeral of a four-year-old boy who had been killed in an accident. I learned that neither the mother nor father was a Christian. In the funeral service I tried to be of comfort to them. I told them that maybe God had called the lamb to him that the sheep might follow. I tried to say that maybe God in this way was calling them to him. I told them that surely God has some purpose in it all. Later, as we turned away from the freshly-made grave in the cemetery, that mother came to me and said, "I understand it now. I know why God took my little boy away. I have not been a Christian, but now I am going to church. I am going to give my heart to the Lord. I am going to live for him. I want to see my baby again one day."

II. God's Secret Plans

We don't understand why God took your baby, but we know he never makes a mistake. He has his secret plans that go on for you and me. And his plans are always best. So this is not the time to question his judgments. It is the time to trust him, knowing that he wouldn't do anything that would permanently hurt you. The hurt is there now, but someday, when all things are made clear and plain, you will know that "all things," even this, "work together for good to them that love God."

When you look at the back of a tapestry you see many colored threads in a maze of confusion. But when you turn the tapestry over you see all the colors gathered together and blended into a beautiful picture. Today we are looking at the back side of the weaving. There are some black threads mingled with the others and we see no beauty there. But someday, when we are with Jesus, we will see that God was working everything together for our good and his glory. You who loved this little one cannot see this now, but I am sure that you will see it in the sweet by-and-by.

III. Your Comfort in This Hour

1. You are comforted as you remember that you had her for a little while if not for a long time

You are happy that she brightened up your lives for a few years if not for many years. You are saying that it is better to have loved and lost than never to have loved at all. You are surely saying that you are going to love Christ more and live closer to him because he lent you this little one for a little while.

2. You are comforted in remembering that you did your best for her

You gave her the best medical skill that could be found. But it seemed that this was the time for her to leave you, so we will just say with one of old, "The Lord gave and the Lord hath taken away, blessed be the name of the Lord."

3. You are comforted in remembering that you will see her again

Some years ago I was called on to conduct the funeral of a baby girl. The mother was ill and could not leave her bed. When the little white casket was rolled by the bedside so that the mother could have one long last look at the baby, that mother cried out, "Goodbye, my darling, I will never see you again." But putting your trust in Christ, you will never have to say that. Because of him you can see your darling again.

So I bid you come to Jesus with all your sorrow today. Come to him who loved your baby and took her to be with him. Come to him who wept with Mary and Martha and who still sympathizes with those who have a broken heart. Come and let him put his loving arms around you and comfort you.

5

For an Aged Christian

Today I am remembering the first funeral I ever conducted as a young preacher. It was the funeral of a woman 72 years of age, but who had never made any profession of any faith in the Lord Jesus Christ. What a pity to go through life like that, neglecting every opportunity of salvation and spurning all of God's offers of grace.

But what a contrast do we find here today. Here is one who gave her life to Christ as a girl, and who has loved and served him for more than sixty years. Oh, surely all the bells of heaven rang out when she left us and entered that blessed city.

We thank God today for such people. They live among us for a while, they bless our hearts, they make life sweeter and better, then they go out to be with God and to await our coming.

1. We Can Judge People by What They Love

1. She loved the Lord

To her God was not some distant person way off yonder in the blue. He was near to her. He was dear to her. He was her daily Companion. She walked and she talked with the King. She spoke often of her gratitude to him for saving her and for blessing her in so many ways.

2. She loved her church

Because she loved Jesus, she loved his church. That always follows. He put the church down here for us to love in and serve through. It is the only institution he ever founded. If you love Christ, you are going to be faithful to his church.

Nothing except a serious illness kept her from attending church. She was there every time the doors were opened. She never shone in the social world, you never saw her name in the society column. But she gave her time and her talents through her church and she blessed more people by her Christian influence than any number of society people you could name.

3. She loved her pastor

She always referred to him as "my pastor." She loved him because he represented her Lord. She was interested in every preacher and missionary, simply because they were telling others of the Christ whom she adored and served.

4. She loved her Bible

Even during her last illness her Bible was always by her bedside. You sometimes see Bibles twenty-five years old that are as clean as they were the day they were bought. They have not been used. But her Bible was stained with use. Many a tear had fallen on its pages. Many a passage was underscored.

Her Bible was a lamp unto her feet and a light unto her pathway. It was her guide from grace to glory. It was her comfort and her strength.

5. She loved prayer

She believed in all the prayer promises of the Bible. She spent hours in intercessory prayer for many people. She believed that prayer changed things and people. Oh, how blessed are those who have someone like this to pray for them. We would do well to take her as an example in the matter of prayer.

6. She loved her friends

That is the reason why so many of you are present today. She loved you and you know it. Many of you can testify to the strength you gained through that love. Many of you can remember the sweet things she did for you because of that love.

7. She loved her family

She had many children, grandchildren, and even great-grand-children. And she loved them all and prayed for them all. She rejoiced when you did well. She wept when you failed to live up to her teaching.

Her husband died six years ago. She was the light of his life, the strength of his success. Now she is with him again.

Yes, she loved all that was finest and best. And that love does not end on this earth. It is simply magnified and made perfect in heaven. "Now abideth faith, hope and love, these three, but the greatest of these is love."

II. Some Words to Think About

1. Rest

She has suffered much in recent months. She has often been tired and exhausted. But now God has given her rest. "There remaineth a rest to the people of God."

2. Reunion

Those who love God never part for the last time. In the vocabulary of God there is no such word as "good-bye." Because Jesus lives, we too shall live. And in that life which never ends we shall be reunited with those whom we have "loved long since and lost a while."

3. Reward

God not only promises to take us to heaven, but to reward us at the end of the way if we have served well and for his glory. She certainly did just that and Christ will reward her generously. She built her life on genuine things, not the perishing things of this earth. He will give her the best things of heaven because of her faithful service.

4. Remembrance

You loved ones will never forget her. Her memory will always grow fresh and green in your heart. Remembering her and her sweet Christian life you will from now on want to be better Christians and better people. When you see her one day in heaven you will want to say: "Mother, I lived as you taught me and by the example you set."

A certain man's mother lived in his home and was a blessing to him and to his family. Each night as she climbed the steps to her room she would stop on the landing and say, "Good night, I'll see you in the morning." Then one night she passed away in her sleep. The entire family was broken-hearted but they found comfort in remembering her last words, "Good-night, I'll see you in the morning." They knew that when the night had passed away, they would see her in God's blessed morning-time.

So let this be your comfort, that she has just gone on to be with God, where sickness and sorrow can never touch her, and where someday you will see her again and be at home with her and her wonderful Savior.

6

For a Christian Woman

When Dwight L. Moody's baby died, he said to the minister who was to conduct the funeral service, "Let there be no sorrow on this occasion." He knew that he could trust the Lord and that the Lord had done only that which was best. I am sure that we feel the same way as we come for the last service for this dear woman. She has suffered much, but now she has found blessed relief and God has taken her to himself. While it is a time of sorrow for those who loved her, it is a wonderful day for her. So let us today rejoice with her, for she is a thousand times better off than any of us who must stay a little longer in this old world.

I. The Home Prepared

Before Jesus went away he said, "I go to prepare a place for you, and if I go I will come again and receive you unto myself, that where I am there ye may be also." Now Christ kept his promise. He prepared heaven for all who loved and trusted him and our friend is in that blessed home even now.

1. Heaven is a place

Heaven is just as much a place as New York or Chicago. Jesus called it a place and I get much comfort in taking Jesus at his word. He prepared the place with us in mind. Everything there will be for our comfort and enjoyment. At last we shall be fully satisfied. And on every gate and on every mansion in the city we shall read the word, "Welcome."

2. Heaven is a home

There are no perfect homes in this world. We gather our loved ones around us and think we are going to be supremely and perfectly and permanently happy. But death comes in to rob us of a loved one. Or one of those near and dear to us decides to move away to some distant city. Our homes are always being broken up. But God's heavenly home is a complete and permanent home. When we get there nothing can ever break up our homes or mar our happiness.

> A tent or a cottage, why should I care,
> They're building a palace for me over there,
> Tho' exiled from home, yet still may I sing,
> All glory to God, I'm a child of the King.

3. Heaven is a busy place

The thought of just sitting around in heaven, strumming on a harp, is obnoxious to the average person We could never be contented in such a place. We want to be occupied. And I believe that God will give us something to do. He gives us tasks to perform down here, but we can never perform them perfectly. But up there, in our perfect bodies, we will do with ease all that God gives us to do.

The poet puts it this way.

> When earth's last picture is painted, and the tubes are all twisted
>   and dried,
> When the oldest colors have faded, and the youngest critic has
>   died,

We shall rest, and, faith, we shall need it—lie down for an aeon
  or two,
Till the Master of all Good Workmen shall set us to work anew!

And those that were good will be happy: they shall sit in a golden
  chair:
They shall splash at a ten-league canvas with brushes of comets'
  hair!
They shall find real saints to draw from—Magdalene, Peter, and
  Paul;
They shall work for an age at a sitting and never be tired at all!

And only the Master shall praise them, and only the Master shall
  blame;
And no one shall work for money, and no one shall work for
  fame;
But each for the joy of the working, and each, in his separate star,
Shall paint the Thing as he sees It for the God of Things as They
  Are!

4. Heaven is a place of reunion

Oh, isn't it wonderful to know that we will see our loved ones
again? Today certain families continue to observe the old-fash-
ioned custom of a yearly reunion. The members of the family gather
from far and near and have a wonderful time together. But sometimes these occasions are tinged with sorrow, for one who was
present the year before is no longer in the land of the living and
he is greatly missed.

But when we all get to heaven there will be no more death
and no more separation. We will be reunited forever in a glorious fellowship.

II. Some Things Shut Out of Heaven

1. There will be no sickness there

There is so much sickness down here. We build our new hos-
pitals but it seems that all of them are still crowded. Now our friend
has known much sickness and pain down here, but in heaven she

is in the perfect likeness of her Lord and these things can never touch her again. There is a simple statement in Revelation that encourages us greatly. It says that "there shall be no more pain, for the former things are passed away."

2. There will be no sorrow there

Every home knows a hush sometimes when sorrow comes. That sorrow may come from the loss of a loved one, it may come from some great disappointment, it may come as a result of sin. But God shall wipe away all of our tears when we get to heaven and our sorrow will be turned to singing.

3. There will be no lack of anything good in heaven

Many of our needs down here are never met, but in heaven we shall lack nothing. The One who made heaven and earth will supply every need. We will be joint heirs with Jesus of all the good things of heaven. Down here we go into many homes where poverty is known. In heaven there is no poverty—no need of any good thing.

4. There will be no sin in heaven

Since the days of Adam and Eve men have been bothered and hurt by sin. Every one of us has felt its effects. Won't it be wonderful when we will be like Jesus and when we will never be tempted by sin?

5. There will be no separation in heaven

Down here the cruelty of death separates a man and his wife who mean everything to each other. Down here the children are often bereft when their mother goes away. I felt that awful sorrow when my mother died. I was only four years of age and I couldn't understand it all, but over the years I have known the pain of separation.

The Bible tells us that in heaven there will be "no more sea." The sea down here often separates us from our loved ones, but there'll be nothing in heaven to separate us from them.

6. There will be no death in heaven

Death is a monster that breaks our hearts and robs us of our dearest treasures. But there'll be no death in heaven and no grave on the hillsides of glory.

III. The Good Things in Heaven

1. We will have perfect health

Just recall that moment when you felt at your buoyant best and multiply it by a million and you'll know something of how you'll feel in heaven.

2. We will have perfect happiness

The happiness we enjoy down here is often tinged with trouble and disappointment, but we shall enjoy unblighted happiness in heaven.

3. We will have perfect contentment

We are never perfectly contented down here, but in heaven the glow of perfect contentment will never leave us.

4. We will have perfect fellowship in heaven

Fellowship with the saints of old, Moses and David and Paul and John and many others. Fellowship with all the great Christians of the ages. Fellowship with this dear one and all of our loved ones.

5. We will have perfect love in heaven

Drummond says that love is the greatest thing on earth, but love cannot compare with the perfect love of heaven.

6. We will have Jesus in heaven

That's the best part of it all. We have often felt his presence down here. We have heard his voice in the deep recesses of our hearts. But one day our faith will turn to sight and we shall see him. Oh, glorious, blessed moment when we fall at his feet and thank him for bringing us home!

Now I have talked to you about heaven today. This is the present home of our beloved friend who has left us. If she could speak to us today, she would say, "I want this to be your home, too, and it can be if you belong to Jesus."

So, with Christ's peace in our hearts and Christ's hope in our souls, we say good-bye to this beloved one and we will hope to meet her again one day at Jesus' feet, where the sunshine of his love forever shines and where we shall never grow old.

For an Unsaved Person

As we come today to this solemn occasion we are reminded anew that our funeral services are not for the dead but for the living. If the preacher has a mission at this it is to try to bring a measure of comfort to those whose hearts are heavy today. Mr. _____ never joined a church, but we are not to judge the inner secrets of any man's heart. We know not what emotions stirred his soul nor what secret communion he might have had with God.

However, we do know this. We know that our God is a great loving God who never makes a mistake. He always looks upon the heart and he does always that which is right and best. So with confidence we leave our friend today in the hands of a merciful heavenly Father, knowing that God's way is the best and his thoughts far above ours.

I. Let Us Think of Death

1. Death is certain

The Bible teaches us that if Jesus tarries, every one of us must go through the experience called death. But we know this fact from daily observation.

Every day we hear of the inroads death makes. Every paper carries an obituary column. Every funeral director is kept busy. Graves are constantly being opened in all of our cemeteries.

Death stalks the land. Disease kills in spite of the advance of modern medicine. Accidents of all kinds rob us of our friends and loved ones. Death is all around us. Methuselah lived to be 969 years of age, but he died. When man sinned in the Garden of Eden, the death sentence was pronounced on the whole human race. Death comes to the palace and to the hovel, to the good and to the bad, to the young and to the old. Royal doors cannot block his entrance and wealth cannot hold him back.

On every side we see signs of approaching death. The leaves fade away and die and fall from the trees. And day by day we are fading away. As the years go by our eyes grow dim and our steps grow feebler and we know we are on the way to death. Now, knowing death is certain, the most important thing in life is to get ready for it by putting all our faith and trust in Jesus Christ.

2. Death is sometimes sudden

Don't ever think that when you start out a new day, it is certain that you will finish that day. When you begin a journey there is no guarantee that you'll complete it. Life hangs on a slender thread. That thread could break at any minute.

One Sunday night I talked and laughed with a good man at the close of the service. Before I ate breakfast on Monday morning the message came to me that he had died suddenly that very hour as he read the morning paper.

While the solo was being sung a few minutes ago, scores of people died. While I read the Scripture and offered the prayer, many others went out to face God and the judgment. Death could come to some of us before the day ends, although we enjoy good health at this moment. So you see how important it is to prepare for the coming of death.

3. Death is never welcome

When Sidney Lanier, the great southern poet, lay dying, he said that he had a thousand unwritten songs in his heart. And when you and I come to the end of the way there will be many things unfinished, things that must forever go undone.

There are a few people who have been sick so long and who have suffered so much that death comes as a welcome release. But to most of us death is never welcome. But, even though it surprises us in the midst of life's activities, we must remember that it is coming and be ready for it. We must live for God each day just as if we knew that would be our last day.

II. Let Us Think of Life As a Preparation Period

Life is short compared to eternity. But we have plenty of time in life to prepare for death. And God has been so good to us in this respect. He surrounds us with every influence to direct us and lead us to himself.

1. *He gives us an open Bible,* in which we learn the way of life everlasting.
2. *He gives us the church,* where we hear of a hope in Christ, and whose spires point us to heaven.
3. *He gives us a conscience,* which points out our sins and nudges us to the better life.
4. *He gives us the prayers of friends and loved ones.* Surely every man who goes to heaven or hell has at some time had someone praying for him.
5. *He gives us sorrow to bring us to himself.* Often it takes a sorrow to make us realize our desperate need of God.
6. *He gives us the Holy Spirit.* Before Jesus went away he said that he would send the Holy Spirit to convict us of sin, righteousness, and judgment to come. And that blessed Spirit comes to point out our sin and point us to Christ.
7. *He gives us a cross.* The Man who died on that cross died for you and invites you to himself, saying, "Him that cometh to me I will in no wise cast out."

Yes, God is good to us to give us all these things to lead us to salvation. You must climb over them all to be lost.

The hour of death is coming for you and me. It can't be long, it may be soon. So let us remember this fact and apply our hearts unto wisdom. Let us remember that "it is appointed unto man once to die and after that the judgment." And knowing these things, let us put our faith in him whom to know is eternal life, giving to his keeping our lives and our souls for time and eternity.

When John Glenn came back to earth from his triple orbit around the world someone asked him about his fear of death on the journey. And he replied, "Many years ago I made my peace with God and therefore I was not afraid." And if you and I have found that same peace, we need have no fear of death or life, of things present or things to come, for none of these things can separate us from the love of God which is in Christ Jesus our Lord.

Now may God bless and comfort the family and all those who are here gathered today. May you feel the loving arms of Jesus around you and may his peace fill your heart today and in all the tomorrows that are to come.

8

For a Christian Man

The Bible says many wonderful things about the death of a Christian. But the trouble with us is that we don't believe these things. We think of death as an end to all things good. We think of death as a time of separation. We think of it as a hideous monster come to cut off all our joys.

But death for the Christian really is a wonderful thing. Suppose that you were in prison camp where you were persecuted and beaten every day, where bamboo shoots were driven under your fingernails, where you had nothing to eat but a dry crust of stale bread every day, and you had to sleep on the cold, damp ground every night. Then suppose some army friends came in and rescued you and took you to a place of rest and good food and happiness. Wouldn't you consider these rescuers as good friends?

Well, we ought to look upon death in that way. We live in a cruel world, a world of a few joys, but a world of many hardships, injustices, trials, tears, sorrows, and separations. Now when death comes to take us into the presence of the Lord, where we will have perfect health and perfect rest, wouldn't you say that death is, after all, a good friend? We look upon death as an enemy, but really it is one of God's servants who takes us to a better land.

So today we just come together to say good-bye to our friend and to thank God that he is now with Jesus, where sickness and sorrow can never touch him. When Dwight L. Moody lay dying, he said, "Earth is receding, heaven is coming down, and I am going home." Our friend could say the same thing. He has just gone over Jordan, he has just gone home.

I. A Wonderful Text

In Psalm 116:15 we read these words, "Precious in the sight of the LORD is the death of his saints." When a Christian dies it is a matter of concern to the Lord. He knows about every breath that we draw, every pain that we endure, every groan that we utter. It all means something to him. Now our text says, not that death is precious in our sight, but in God's sight. The psalmist is talking about death from God's standpoint.

A young man who was living a faithful Christian life was killed by a drunken driver. When the preacher quoted this text, the boy's mother sobbed out, "I don't see how my boy's death could be precious in God's sight." But she was looking at the matter from a human standpoint, and not from God's.

Whether death comes suddenly or after a lingering illness, whether it comes in war or in peace, whether one is killed accidentally on the highway or dies quietly in bed, it is because God permits it and I believe it is precious in God's sight.

So today the death of this our friend brings grief to us, but it is precious in God's sight.

II. A Wonderful Sleep

The Bible says, "He giveth his beloved sleep." Elizabeth Barrett Browning said that to her this was the sweetest text in the Bible.

Now sleep is a very wonderful thing. We can't do without it. Every living thing must have some time for sleep. It "knits up the raveled sleeve of care." It brings us sweet rest and gives us new strength for the new day. Yes, physical sleep is a wonderful thing, but it can never compare with the sleep God gives to his beloved.

What a different sleep that is, indeed! We go to sleep tonight and when we wake up tomorrow, we have the same old problems and worries and aches and pains that were ours when we went to bed. But when we go to sleep in Jesus, we soon wake up on a new shore and find that it is heaven. We breathe a new air and find that it is celestial air. We feel the touch of a new hand on ours and find that it is God's hand.

III. The Meaning of Death for a Christian

1. It means a change of environment

Everything down here has been contaminated by sin. On every hand we find dishonesty, drunkenness, lies, and lust. And we also find all the by-products of sin, namely sickness, sorrow, pain, poverty, and death.

But when God's people die they go to a place where these things can never touch them. There is for them a complete change of environment. They go from sin to sinlessness, from earth's hovels to heaven's mansions, from earth's discords to heaven's harmonies, from all that is bad to all that is good, from all that hurts to all that brings happiness.

2. It means a change of nature

Here we are burdened with an old carnal nature, that causes us continual grief. Up there the old sinful, fleshly nature will be gone forever. "This robe of flesh I'll drop and rise to seize the everlasting prize."

3. It means a reunion with our loved ones

You have stood by the bedside and watched your loved ones die. You have looked into their faces for the last time and wept many bitter tears. But they are not gone from you forever. You will see them again in a land of light and love.

My wife and I some years ago took a wonderful trip to Hawaii. When we returned and our ship docked at San Francisco there were hundreds of people there to meet their loved ones. The band was playing and people were rushing up and throwing their arms around their loved ones who had been away. But we didn't know anyone in San Francisco, so there was no one there to greet us. It's going to be different when the old ship Zion pulls into heaven. Our loved ones and our friends and our Savior will be there to greet us and welcome us to the heavenly city.

4. It means that we will see Jesus

If it were not for him there would be no heaven. The golden streets and the pearly gates and the mansions and the robes and the crowns would mean absolutely nothing if Jesus were not there. But, thank God, we shall see him and we shall know him and we shall want to fall at his feet and thank him for saving us and bringing us safely home.

So now as we say "good-bye" to this beloved friend, we realize how wonderful it is up there for him. May his memory linger on in our hearts to bless us and bring us closer to God.

We live in a great and growing city. There are many fast-growing cities in the land. But the city that is growing faster than all others is the holy city of the New Jerusalem, which we call heaven. May God grant that we might so live and so trust Christ that someday we, too, shall join this friend in that wonderful city.

Sleep on, beloved, sleep, and take thy rest;
Lay down thy head upon thy Savior's breast;
We love thee well, but Jesus loves thee best—
Good-night! Good-night! Good-night!

Calm is thy slumber as an infant's sleep;
But thou shall not wake no more to toil and weep;
Thine is a perfect rest secure and deep—
Good-night! Good-night! Good-night!

Until the Easter glory lights the skies,
Until the dead in Jesus shall arise,
And he shall come, but in lowly guise—
Good-night! Good-night! Good-night!

Until made beautiful by Love Divine,
Thou, in the likeness of thy Lord shalt shine,
And He shall bring that golden crown of thine—
Good-night! Good-night! Good-night!

Only "Good-night," beloved—not "farewell"!
A little while and all His saints shall dwell
In hallowed union indivisible—
Good-night! Good-night! Good-night!

For a Christian

Someone pictured death in this way: A little child is playing late in the evening with some children. They mistreat him and abuse him. He becomes weary and sick at heart. Then a kind nurse comes and takes him home. She places him in bed, tucks the covers around him, and soon he drifts off into peaceful slumber. Death is that kind nurse. God sends him down to snatch us away from the hardships of life and give us eternal rest.

Listen to what the Bible says about death: "Blessed are the dead which die in the Lord from henceforth: Yea, saith the Spirit, that they may rest from their labors; and their works do follow them" (Rev. 14:13); "Absent from the body, . . . present with the Lord" (2 Cor. 5:8); "He giveth his beloved sleep" (Ps. 127:2); and "For me to live is Christ, and to die is gain" (Phil. 1:21).

Listen to Paul as he approaches death: "I have fought a good fight, I have finished my course, I have kept the faith: henceforth there is laid up for me a crown of righteousness, which the Lord, the righteous judge, shall give me at that day: and not to me only, but unto all them also that love his appearing" (2 Tim. 4:7–8).

I am not saying that death is a pretty thing. It hurts us to stand by and see our loved ones suffer and die. Yet remember this: While our own hearts are breaking, our loved ones have gone up to meet Jesus and to receive all the wonderful things he has in store for them.

Now we come to this wonderful text, "Precious in the sight of the LORD is the death of his saints" (Ps. 116:15). When a Christian dies, it is not a matter of indifference to the Lord. He knows about every pain, every breath that is drawn, every groan that is uttered. All of it means something to him. The text does not say that death is precious in our sight, but in God's sight. It speaks of death from God's viewpoint.

A young preacher married a fine girl, but within three months she died. The preacher who conducted the funeral quoted Romans 8:28. The young preacher said, "I know that's in the Bible, but I can't see how it's true in my case." He was looking at the matter from a human standpoint and not from God's.

In 1973 my eldest son died. It seemed that he had everything to live for when God took him. I do not understand it because I look at it from the human viewpoint. But if I could see his death from God's viewpoint, I know I would see it was for the best.

Whether in war or peace, whether death comes suddenly or after a lingering illness, whether on a busy highway or in a quiet bedroom, I believe it comes because God permits it and that it is precious in his sight.

I. The Death of a Child of God Means a Change of Environment

We live in an environment of sin. The best Christian is surrounded by it; the best home is contaminated by it. On every hand there is sin in some form. Every form of sin characterizes our environment. But in heaven there is a complete change. No more do we rub elbows with dishonesty, drunkenness, lies, lust, or any other sin. Instead of being surrounded by sinners, we associate with the angels, with the redeemed of all ages, and with the Lord Jesus Christ himself.

Think of the by-products of sin: sickness, sorrow, pain, poverty, broken hearts and homes, death. These came into the world because of sin. But when God's people die, they go to a place where there is never any sickness, sorrow, trouble, or pain. No more operations, no more weeping, no more funerals. No wonder a Christian's death is precious in God's sight. He knows that person is safe from all these things.

There is an old, old debate that has never been settled, "Which is stronger, heredity or environment?" I believe environment is the stronger. Take a child from ungodly parents when he is one day old, give him to Christian parents, let them bring him up in a godly home, and I believe he will probably become more good than bad. But take a child from a Christian couple when he is one day old, give him to a godless, drunken, profane couple, and let them bring him up in that atmosphere. I am sure he will more probably turn out bad rather than good. Yes, environment is a mighty power, because we live in a world where the devil is so active, where sin and its by-products press down on us.

But what a change when we get to heaven! We go from sin to sinlessness, from earth's hovels to heaven's mansions, from earth's discords to heaven's harmony, from all that is bad to all that is good, from all that hurts to all that brings happiness. No wonder the death of a saint, a child of God, is precious in God's sight.

When Sir Walter Raleigh was put to death, he was as serene and calm as a June morning. Running his finger over the axe to be used in beheading him, he said, "This is a sharp medic but it is a cure for all diseases." Yes, death cures all our diseases and changes our environment from gloom to glory.

II. The Death of a Child of God Means a Change of Nature

In this life we are all burdened with a carnal, sinful, fleshly nature. It causes us continual grief; it is always getting us into trouble. We don't want to sin—that's the spiritual nature within us. But we do go ahead and sin—that's the old carnal nature within us.

Simon Peter loved Jesus, but one night he lied. He said he didn't know Jesus, and he punctuated his denial with an oath. Then Jesus looked at him and that one look broke Peter's heart. He went out and wept bitterly. His denial was a result of his carnal or sinful nature, which was always a burden to him. Paul was the great apostle, but he said, "The things I want to do, I do not; the things I ought not to do, I do." He said it was because of the sinful nature that dwelt within him.

David was a man after God's own heart, but he sinned greatly. When he repented, he said that God was breaking his bones. David did not mean this literally—he was using a figure of speech. He really meant he was as miserable as if all his bones were broken. He had allowed his old carnal nature to get the upper hand.

This is the experience of every Christian. We know Christ, and deep down in our hearts we want to be good and do good. But that old sinful nature is still with us. It drags us down, makes us weep, and becomes a burden to us.

But when we die there is a change of nature. The old nature is gone forever. As the song says:

> This robe of flesh I'll drop and rise
> To seize the everlasting prize.

It will be wonderful when there is nothing in us to drag us down and make us do and say evil things. We'll be like that when we meet Jesus. Whether we die or are caught up in the air, the result will be the same. Whether we go by the undertaker or the "upper-taker," we'll leave our old, sinful, carnal, fleshly natures behind.

III. The Death of a Child of God Proves the Reality of Our Religion

Some Christians live in such a way that the world doubts the reality of their religion. But when a true Christian dies, he testifies to the presence and reality of religion. The Lord is never quite so close as in the hour of death. John Wesley said, "Our people die well." He was simply saying that Christ is real in that hour.

Stephen was stoned to death. While Paul watched over the cloaks of the stoners, he heard Stephen say, "Lord, lay not this sin to their charge." Paul never forgot Stephen's words and his attitude. They prepared him for his conversion. He must have said, "If a man can die like that, there must be something to the Christian religion."

Polycarp was a great Christian in the early church. He was condemned to die by burning, but was promised his life if he would renounce Christ. He said, "Eighty and six years have I served him and he has never wronged me. How can I forsake him now?" They burned his body, but his soul went to be with God. Men don't die like that unless Christianity is a reality to them.

IV. The Death of a Child of God Draws Christians Nearer to Him

In Numbers 23:10 we read, "Let me die the death of the righteous, and let my last end be like his!" This man had seen a godly man die and how the Lord was with him. He too wanted to die like that.

A certain man was a Christian, but not a very faithful one. One day his son, whom he loved greatly, died suddenly. The night after the funeral he began to read his Bible. He took a red pencil and marked every verse that spoke of heaven, where his son had gone. This Bible reading brought him closer to God. His son's death had drawn him closer to God.

I conducted a meeting in Athens, Georgia. On Sunday night my brother called from our old home-place. He said, "You had better come home if you want to see papa alive." I drove the twenty-four miles and sat by my father's bedside until he died the next morning. One of my brothers and I went into the next room, and through his tears my brother said, "It makes you want to live a better life, doesn't it?" And certainly it is true that when one of our loved ones goes to be with God we are brought closer to him.

V. The Death of a Child of God Means a Welcome Home for Him

This world is not our home. The years we spend here are nothing compared to eternity. Our citizenship is in heaven, and before long we will be going to our home.

We once lived in a little town nestled among the hills of western North Carolina. Often we would go away from home, but we always looked forward to getting back. Several miles out of town we would come to the top of a hill. From it we could look down on the little town. We were always glad when we reached that spot because it meant we were almost home. Someday on the highway of life we're going to come to that last hill, and the saints and angels and the blessed Jesus will be waiting to welcome us home.

Some years ago my wife and I took a trip to Hawaii. When the ship docked in San Francisco, hundreds of people were there to welcome their loved ones. The band was playing and many relatives and friends rushed forward to welcome their loved ones back home. But there was no one there to meet us, for we didn't know anyone in San Francisco. But it's going to be different when the old ship Zion pulls into glory. Loved ones and friends and the Savior whom we've tried to serve will be there to welcome us into the heavenly city.

A native preacher of Africa said, "When a heathen is dying, the witch doctor puts a dead bone in his hand as a passport into another land. When a Christian dies, he doesn't grasp a dead bone, but the hand of the living Lord." Yes, thank God, when we come to the end of the journey, the Lord himself will welcome us home.

A preacher stood by the bedside of a dying saint. This godly woman called her children in one by one and told them good-bye. Then she asked the preacher to read Psalm 90 and the passages in Revelation about heaven. He did so and then she said, "The angels are at the foot of the bed. They've come for me." She fell asleep to wake up in the presence of the King.

Don't you want to die like that? Don't you want to go to heaven at the end of the way? Then put your trust in the Lord Jesus Christ. Your death will be precious in God's sight, and you can say with Paul, "For me to live is Christ, and to die is gain."

The W. Herschel Ford Sermon Library

These are sermons that preachers can preach, that teachers can teach, that students can study, and that God's people can read with boundless profit. . . . Anyone who would open his mind and soul to these beautifully worded, magnificently outlined expositions of the truth of God will be gloriously blessed.

W. A. Criswell
Pastor, First Baptist Church
Dallas, Texas

The following titles are now available in the W. Herschel Ford Sermon Library:

Simple Sermons for Funeral Services (0-8010-9122-5)
Simple Sermons for Special Days and Occasions (0-8010-9121-7)
Simple Sermons on Great Christian Doctrines (0-8010-9124-1)
Simple Sermons on Prayer (0-8010-9125-X)
Simple Sermons for Sunday Morning (0-8010-9120-9)
Simple Sermons on Salvation and Service (0-8010-9123-3)